WHERE'S WALLY?
THE WILDLY WONDERFUL
ACTIVITY BOOK

Based on the characters created by
MARTIN HANDFORD

WALKER BOOKS
AND SUBSIDIARIES
LONDON • BOSTON • SYDNEY

WELCOME, WALLY-WATCHERS.

I'M JUST SETTING OUT ON A WILDLY WONDERFUL JOURNEY! FOLLOW ME THROUGH THE PAGES OF THIS BOOK, FROM UNDER THE SEA TO OUTER SPACE, FROM A STONE AGE CAVE TOWN TO THE WACKY WILD WEST.

AS WELL AS FINDING ME IN EVERY PICTURE, O FAITHFUL SEEKERS OF WALLY, THERE ARE AN AMAZING NUMBER OF THINGS TO DO ON THE WAY — GAMES TO PLAY, TONGUE-TWISTERS TO SAY, RIDDLES TO SOLVE AND FACTS TO LEARN. WOOF AND WIZARD WHITEBEARD APPEAR ONCE EACH AND I WILL LEAVE A STRIPED SOCK AND A STRIPED TIE FOR YOU TO PICK UP. I AM ALSO TAKING 11 BANANAS WITH ME — CAN YOU FIND THEM ALL, OR AT LEAST THEIR SKINS?

THERE IS ONE MORE TASK TO TELL YOU ABOUT. SOMEWHERE ON EACH PAGE IS A CHARACTER OR OBJECT THAT BELONGS TO ANOTHER SCENE IN THE BOOK. CAN YOU SPOT THE MISFITS AND FIND WHICH PICTURES THEY COME FROM?

THE ANSWERS TO ALL THE RIDDLES AND PUZZLES ARE IN THE BACK, BUT NO CHEATING! AND IF YOU ARE NOT TOO EXHAUSTED, EACH PAGE HAS ITS OWN CHECK LIST OF 10 THINGS TO FIND.

OK WALLY-WATCHERS, GRAB YOUR BINOCULARS, PICK UP YOUR WALKING STICK AND LET'S GET WANDERING.

Wally

DINOSAUR GAMES

DID YOU KNOW?

Dinosaurs actually roamed the earth for 165 million years before they became extinct.

The largest dinosaur was the Brachiosaurus. It weighed about the same as 20 elephants.

In some places archaeologists have discovered 2 sets of dinosaur tracks next to each other which may mean that some dinosaurs used to walk side by side for company.

THINGS TO DO

How many different words can you make out of:

TYRANNOSAURUS REX

Rating: 20, good; 30, very good; more than 50, truly astonishing!

Try saying this tongue-twister as fast as you can:
Tiny Timmy Tyrannosaurus took the train to Transylvania.

Why did the dinosaur cross the road?
Because the chicken hadn't been invented.

AMAZING!
HAVE YOU EVER SEEN SUCH A
COLLECTION OF DIPPY DINOS? I HAD
NO IDEA THEY HAD SUCH FUN AND GAMES.
TALKING OF GAMES, THERE'S SOMETHING IN
THIS PICTURE THAT'S GOT LOST IN TIME.
IT LOOKS LIKE AN EGG
LAID IN A NEST,
BUT IT'S YELLOW AND ROUND
AND WON'T HATCH
LIKE THE REST.

THIS DAFT DINO IS MADE OF
BITS FROM 6 REAL DINOSAURS.
CAN YOU RECOGNIZE ALL
OF THEM?

MEDIEVAL MAYHEM

DID YOU KNOW?

Some medieval castles have murder-holes through which sharp or heavy objects could be dropped from a great height on to enemies below.

Many castles have spiral staircases. Next time you visit an ancient castle notice how they always spiral up clockwise – the central pillar stopped anyone going up being able to brandish a sword properly.

THINGS TO DO

Can you find these 6 medieval words on the grid?

Turret
Spear
Moat
Shield
Keep
Tunic

T	O	L	S	E	M	P
U	S	O	H	C	O	G
R	O	P	I	K	A	B
R	U	N	E	R	T	L
E	U	E	L	A	S	R
T	P	H	D	I	R	D

What's the definition of attack?

A small nail.

WOW! THIS MEDIEVAL MAYHEM IS ENOUGH TO DRIVE ANYONE UP THE WALL. CAN YOU FIND ME IN THIS KNIGHT-TIME CHAOS, AND WHAT ABOUT THIS WEAPON THAT REALLY BELONGS IN THE KITCHEN? IT FLATTENS THE PASTRY, IT'S YELLOW AND ROUND, IT COULD KNOCK YOU OUT AS IT FALLS TO THE GROUND.

ALL BUT ONE OF THESE LITTLE PICTURES CAN BE FOUND IN THE MAIN SCENE. CAN YOU SPOT WHICH IS THE ODD ONE OUT?

A
B
C
D
E

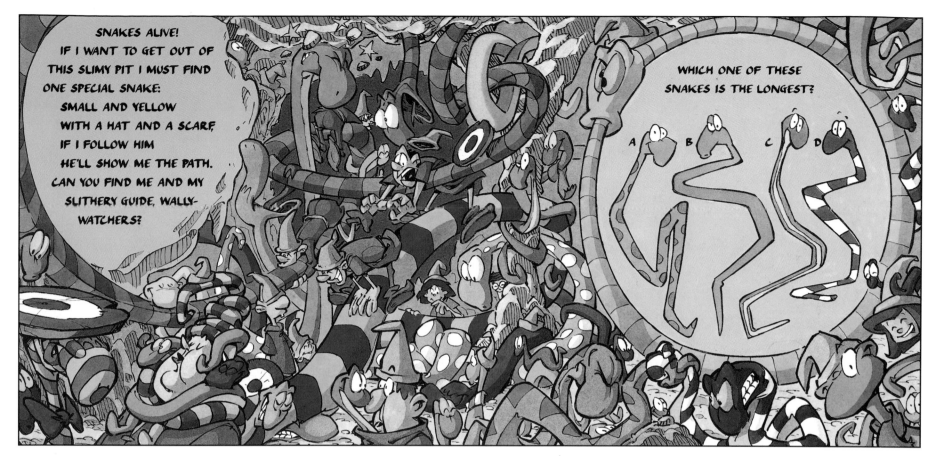

SNAKE PIT

DID YOU KNOW?

One of the biggest snakes ever found was an Anaconda. It was 8.45 metres long with a girth of 111 centimetres.

Most pythons kill their prey by constricting or squeezing it, and the larger species can swallow animals as big as goats and pigs.

Snakes grow continuously throughout their lives, shedding their skins when they outgrow them.

THINGS TO DO

How many different snakes can you read here?

Why can you never play a trick on a snake?

Because you can't pull its leg.

WHAT A SPECTACULAR SCENE, WALLY-WATCHERS, STUFFED
FULL OF YOUR FAVOURITE STARS, EACH WANTING TO TAKE
THE LEAD. I WOULDN'T WANT THE TASK OF DIRECTING THIS
BOISTEROUS BUNCH. MIND YOU, IF SOMEBODY DOESN'T STOP
THAT ELEPHANT THERE WON'T BE A FILM TO DIRECT.
THERE ARE LOTS OF CHARACTERS TO SPOT HERE, BUT
FIRST CAN YOU FIND THIS PROP:

WHEN A SCENE NEEDS A TUNE
YOU CAN USE ONE OF THESE.
IT'S WHITE AND SINGS
WHEN YOU PLAY WITH THE KEYS.
WHEN YOU'VE SOLVED THE RIDDLE SEE IF YOU CAN LEAD
THE FILM EDITOR TO THE DIRECTOR IN THE MAZE
OPPOSITE. AND DON'T FORGET TO LOOK FOR ME.
I LIKE TO STAY IN THE PICTURE. HAPPY HUNTING.

FILM SET

DID YOU KNOW?

Hollywood, in California, became a centre for film making because the weather is nearly always good and there is a wide variety of scenery – from deserts to tropical islands.

The character most often portrayed on film is Sherlock Holmes. The character most often portrayed in horror films is Count Dracula.

The country which has made the most feature films is India.

THINGS TO DO

The names of some famous film characters have been split up. Can you find 5 whole names among these bits? What piece of film-making equipment can you make from the remaining pieces?

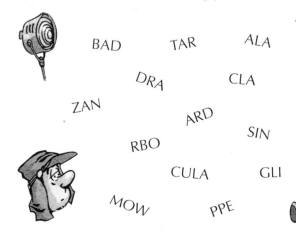

BAD   TAR   ALA

DRA   CLA

ZAN

ARD   DDIN

SIN

RBO

CULA   GLI

MOW   PPE

How did Frankenstein eat his food?

ʻumop ʇı pǝʇloq ǝH

ICE-CREAM PARTY

DID YOU KNOW?

The Chinese probably invented ice-cream. They used to eat snow mixed with lemons, oranges or pomegranates.

The record for ice-cream eating is over 9 litres in 8 minutes.

The largest ice-cream ever was a sundae made in Canada in 1988. It weighed nearly 25 kg, including syrup and topping.

THINGS TO DO

Here are 4 favourite pudding combinations. The first parts are given, but three letter clues to the second parts are written in the cubes. Can you work out what the complete puddings are?

Strawberries and [c r a]   Pancakes and [r s p]

Jelly and [m c e]   Bananas and [a s d]

How does a monster count to 19?

On his fingers.

THESE ICE-CREAM LOVERS ARE TRYING TO WORK OUT WHICH COMBINATION OF FLAVOURS THEY ALL LIKE THE BEST.
A LONG YELLOW FRUIT THAT'S EASY TO SLICE, PLUS FINE ORANGE JAM THAT ON TOAST IS QUITE NICE.

CAN YOU UNJUMBLE THE UNUSUAL ICE-CREAM FLAVOURS ON THESE BOTTLES?

SPAR PIN

LICOROBC

TAM OTO

GEBACAB

RAC TOR

WOW! IF THIS SCENE IS ANYTHING TO GO BY, LIFE WAS CERTAINLY NOT DULL BACK IN THE STONE AGE. I PREDICT A COMPLETELY CALAMITOUS CATASTROPHE IN A SECOND. IT MAY LOOK TINY BUT...
LOOK AT THE MAMMOTH, HE'S IN FOR A SHOCK; WHEN HE PUTS HIS FOOT DOWN, THE WHOLE CAVE WILL ROCK.

LOOK AT THE JUMBLED LETTERS BELOW. DELETE THOSE THAT APPEAR TWICE AND USE THE REST TO WORK OUT THE NAME OF THIS STONE AGE STREET

S M O G E
K C T R N
S P E I D
N G B A S
T L E P F

--- / ----- / STREET

LPBGETNSP

CAVE RAVE

DID YOU KNOW?

Neanderthal Man lived between 35,000 and 100,000 years ago. Fossil remains were found near the River Neander in Germany.

Although mammoths are now extinct we know a great deal about them as they were well preserved in the frozen ground of Northern Europe. Most mammoths were as big as elephants and were covered in long, shaggy hair.

THINGS TO DO

Try saying this tongue-twister as fast as you can:

Micky Mammoth met a massive monkey.
Did Micky Mammoth meet a massive monkey?
If Micky Mammoth met a massive monkey
Where's the massive monkey Micky met?

Is it hard to bury a dead mammoth?
Yes, it's a huge undertaking.

DRAGON RIDE

DID YOU KNOW?

Dragons are entirely mythical creatures but they appear in the ancient cultures of many countries throughout the world.

The legends about dragons developed long before man had any knowledge of prehistoric animals.

Our word "dragon" comes from the Greek word *drakon*, which was used to describe any large serpent.

THINGS TO DO

Can you fill in the grid of mythical beasts using the central word and clues to help you?

1. Snake-headed woman
2. Half woman half fish
3. Half man half goat
4. Flying horse
5. White horse with one long horn
6. Half man half bull

What kind of plane does a dragon fly?

M	E	D	U	S	A	
M	E	R	M	A	I	D
	S	A	T	Y	R	
P	E	G	A	S	U	S
U	N	I	C	O	R	N
M	I	N	A	T	O	U	R

A Spitfire.

PHEW! I'VE GOT A GOOD VIEW OVER A CROWDED SKY, BUT I CAN'T GO HOME UNTIL I FIND THIS VALUABLE OBJECT:

MY FIRST IS IN KETTLE,
MY SECOND IN TEA,
MY THIRD IS IN YELLOW,
THE COLOUR OF ME.

THESE 5 HAPPY HUNTERS ALL SEEM TO BE THE SAME BUT 2 OF THEM ARE DIFFERENT. CAN YOU SPOT WHICH ONES?

A
B
C
D
E

A FEAST OF PIES

DID YOU KNOW?

The biggest cake ever made weighed over 58 tonnes, including 7.35 tonnes of icing.

The oldest cake in the world is over 4,000 years old. It was vacuum-packed in an Egyptian grave in 2200 BC.

The longest loaf of bread ever made was 718.67 m long.

THINGS TO DO

Model your own Wally face by using this recipe to make salt dough: Mix together 100g plain flour, 150g salt, a dessertspoon of cooking oil and enough water to make a stretchy dough. Knead it until smooth and shape your model. Bake the dough in a cool oven for 2 – 3 hours until hard. When it is quite cold, colour your model with paints or felt-tip pens. This is not an edible recipe!

What looks just like half a loaf of bread? ʇlɐɥ ɹǝɥʇo ǝɥ⊥

WOW! HOW ABOUT THIS FOR A FUN-FILLED FLIGHT OF FANCY? THIS IS THE BALLOON RACE OF A LIFETIME! I HOPE ALL THIS FLOATING AROUND DOESN'T MAKE YOU LIGHT-HEADED! UNBELIEVABLE! THERE GOES AN ALIEN IN A YELLOW ROCKET. CAN YOU SEE HIM TOO? AND WHAT ABOUT A MAGIC CARPET, A KNIGHT IN ARMOUR AND A MESSAGE IN A BOTTLE?

I SAW THE STRANGEST SIGHT OF ALL JUST NOW. HERE'S A CLUE TO HELP YOU SPOT WHAT IT WAS:

HE'S GREEN AND HE'S CROAKING;
BELIEVE ME, IT'S TRUE!
HE'S SITTING IN WATER,
ADMIRING THE VIEW!

BETTER CATCH HIM BEFORE HE GOES UP, UP AND AWAY. AS EACH BALLOON ENTERED THE RACE THEY WERE GIVEN A NUMBER. THE VERY LAST COMPETITOR, THE ONE WITH THE HIGHEST NUMBER APPEARS IN THIS PICTURE.
CAN YOU FIND IT?

BALLOON RACE

DID YOU KNOW?

Joseph and Étienne Montgolfier launched a hot air balloon on 19th September 1783 which carried a sheep, a cockerel and a duck. It flew for 8 minutes.

On 21st November 1783 Francois Laurent and Jean François Pilâtre de Rozier were the first people to sail in a hot air balloon. They sailed over Paris for about 9 km and burned wool and straw to keep the air in the balloon hot.

Napoleon used hot air balloons as anchored observation points in some of his battles.

THINGS TO DO

Invincible balloon
Did you know that if you place a piece of sticky-tape over a blown-up balloon and then stick a pin through the tape, the balloon will not burst! Try it yourself and see!

Water-bending balloon trick
Turn on a cold water tap. Rub a blown-up balloon on your sleeve and then hold it next to the running water (but don't let the balloon actually touch the water). See how the balloon static bends the water.

What did the balloon say to the pin? ¡Hi buster!

ONLY 5 OF THESE PICTURES
CAN BE FOUND IN OUR HOT AIR SCENE.
CAN YOU SPOT THE ODD ONE OUT?

WHEN YOU'VE FOUND THE ONE THAT
DOESN'T FIT, LOOK THROUGH THE REST OF THE
BOOK TO DISCOVER WHICH INCREDIBLE WALLY SCENE
IT BELONGS TO:

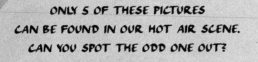

A   B   C

D   E   F

PHEW! I DON'T KNOW ABOUT YOU BUT
I'M GETTING CARRIED AWAY - THIS
IS SUCH AN UPLIFTING
EXPERIENCE! !

PIRATES AHOY

DID YOU KNOW?

There have been pirates in history as far back as Greek and Roman times.

Pirates were often recruited from naval crews who were no longer needed for war.

Many sixteenth century galleons carried cannons which could shoot nearly 15 kg of shot.

THINGS TO DO

In the mayhem these pirates tore up a scroll containing clues to hidden treasure. Each clue was ripped in half. Can you put them back together? To find out where the treasure lies, take the first word of the first sentence, the second of the second and so on.

1 It's easy	the anchor.
2 Look in	to find.
3 Then weigh	crow's flying.
4 See how the	a gull's nest.
5 And find	the hold.

Why does the sea never fall over the horizon?   *It's tide.*

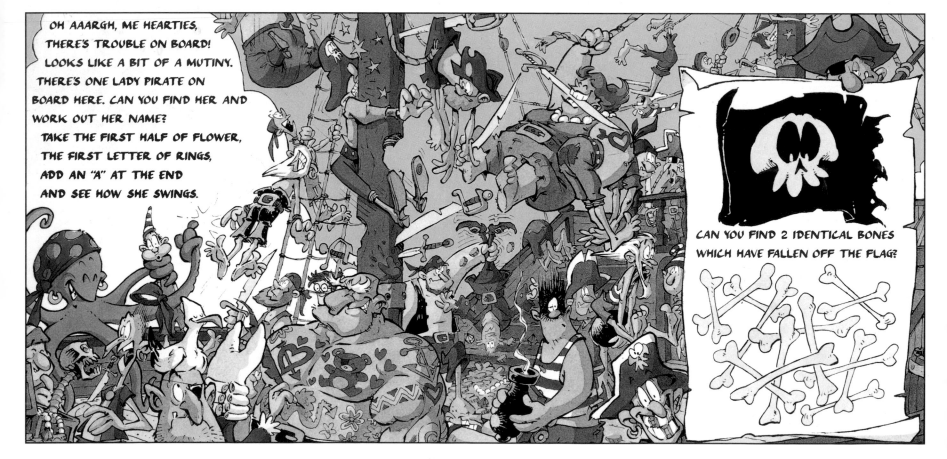

OH AAARGH, ME HEARTIES, THERE'S TROUBLE ON BOARD! LOOKS LIKE A BIT OF A MUTINY. THERE'S ONE LADY PIRATE ON BOARD HERE. CAN YOU FIND HER AND WORK OUT HER NAME? TAKE THE FIRST HALF OF FLOWER, THE FIRST LETTER OF RINGS, ADD AN "A" AT THE END AND SEE HOW SHE SWINGS.

CAN YOU FIND 2 IDENTICAL BONES WHICH HAVE FALLEN OFF THE FLAG?

CUPID CHAOS

DID YOU KNOW?

Cupid was the Roman god of love. He was often drawn as a child with wings, carrying a bow and arrow. Whoever he hit was destined to fall in love, but Cupid was blind and often made mistakes!

St Valentine's Day is on 14th February. It is the day when lovers send each other messages, often written in code or disguised handwriting to keep the loved one guessing. It is thought that Valentine's cards were the first greetings cards ever sent.

THINGS TO DO

Can you crack this saying, written in code. The clue is in every other letter:

ERLOENPDHGALNSTTSI
NBEOVTERRY
FXOFRHGNELT

Why did the cockerel fall in love with the hen?

She egged him on.

SNOWSTORM

DID YOU KNOW?

Snowflakes are always hexagonal.
That means they always have 6 sides.

In September 1981 the temperature in the Kalahari Desert in Africa dropped to 5°C and for the first time in living memory there was snow in the desert.

The biggest snowman ever was over 19 metres high and took a team 2 weeks to build. They called him Super Frosty.

THINGS TO DO

Can you lift an ice cube with a match?
Rest a used match on top of an ice cube.
Sprinkle it with salt, wait a few moments and lift up the cube with the match.
Easy!

How do you make anti-freeze?

Hide her nightie.

IT'S SNOW JOKE! THESE SNOWMEN ARE COMPLETELY OUT OF CONTROL, AND SOMEONE HAS BEEN PLAYING A PRACTICAL JOKE ON ONE OF THEM. CAN YOU SPOT WHO IT IS?
HE LOOKS MOST PECULIAR;
HE'LL NEED HELP WHEN HE'S FOUND.
ONE PART OF HIS BODY
IS THE WRONG WAY AROUND.

WHICH 3 PIECES FIT TOGETHER TO MAKE THE COMPLETE SNOW HEAD?

A
B
C
D
E
F

In the top illustration speech bubbles read:

LOOK AT ALL THESE STARRY-EYED ASTRONOMERS, WALLY-WATCHERS. CAN YOU SPOT 2 HAPPY STAR GAZERS? WHIZZING THROUGH SPACE IN THEIR SHIP MADE FOR 2, THEY LOOK JUST THE SAME BUT ONE'S PINK AND ONE'S BLUE.

START AT THE RED ARROW AND FIND A WAY THROUGH THE MAZE TO THE WHITE STAR.

STAR GAZING

DID YOU KNOW?

There are trillions of stars in the universe but only 5,780 are visible from Earth without a telescope.

The very centre of a star is extremely hot. It can reach a temperature of 16 million °C.

The longest name of any star is *Shurnarkabishashututu*. It is Arabic for "under the southern horn of the bull".

THINGS TO DO

Here is a martian signpost. Can you work out what it says by using the code-breaker? Read the grid across first then up to get each letter.

	A	B	C	D	E
	F	G	H	I	J
	K	L	M	N	O
	P	Q	R	S	T
	U	V	W	X	Y/Z

What's a spaceman's favourite game?

Astronaughts and crosses.

DEEP SEA DIVING

DID YOU KNOW?

All sorts of weird and wonderful creatures live on the bottom of the deep sea bed. It's so dark down there that some fish make themselves glow with light to attract prey, confuse an enemy or find a mate.

The octopus is thought to be the most intelligent of all invertebrates. When in danger it squirts out ink to make a screen to hide behind.

THINGS TO DO

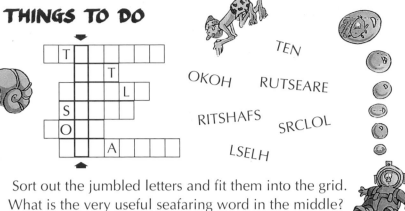

TEN

OKOH   RUTSEARE

RITSHAFS   SRCLOL

LSELH

Sort out the jumbled letters and fit them into the grid. What is the very useful seafaring word in the middle?

How does an octopus go into battle?

Well armed.

WELCOME, WALLY-WATCHERS, TO THE WISHY-WASHY WORLD OF UNDER THE SEA. I'VE BEEN HAVING A FANTASTIC FLIPPER-FLAPPING TIME DOWN HERE BUT NOW ITS TIME TO GO HOME. IF YOU CAN HELP ME SOLVE THIS RIDDLE I WILL GET A LIFT BACK TO DRY LAND:

IT'S A CRAFT FOR EXPLORING THE DEEP SEA BED, AND A PERISCOPE HELPS SEE THE WAY UP AHEAD.

THESE 2 HAPPY SEAHORSES SEEM TO BE IDENTICAL TWINS AT FIRST, BUT LOOK CAREFULLY - THERE ARE 6 DIFFERENCES TO SPOT. CAN YOU FIND THEM ALL?

WILD WEST HEROES

THINGS TO DO

Can you match the silhouettes to the right objects in the picture, and spot the odd one out?

The odd shape out comes from another picture in the book; can you find which one?

Where do cowboys keep their water supply?
In their ten gallon hats.

DID YOU KNOW?

The era of the cowboy was the nineteenth century when beef was a profitable business in America. A herd of 2,500 cattle was looked after by 8 to 12 cowboys. It was Hollywood that gave cowboys their tough image.

Rodeos are competitions in which cowboys show off their skills. One of the best known exhibitions is the bucking bronco when a rider tries to stay on an unbroken horse.

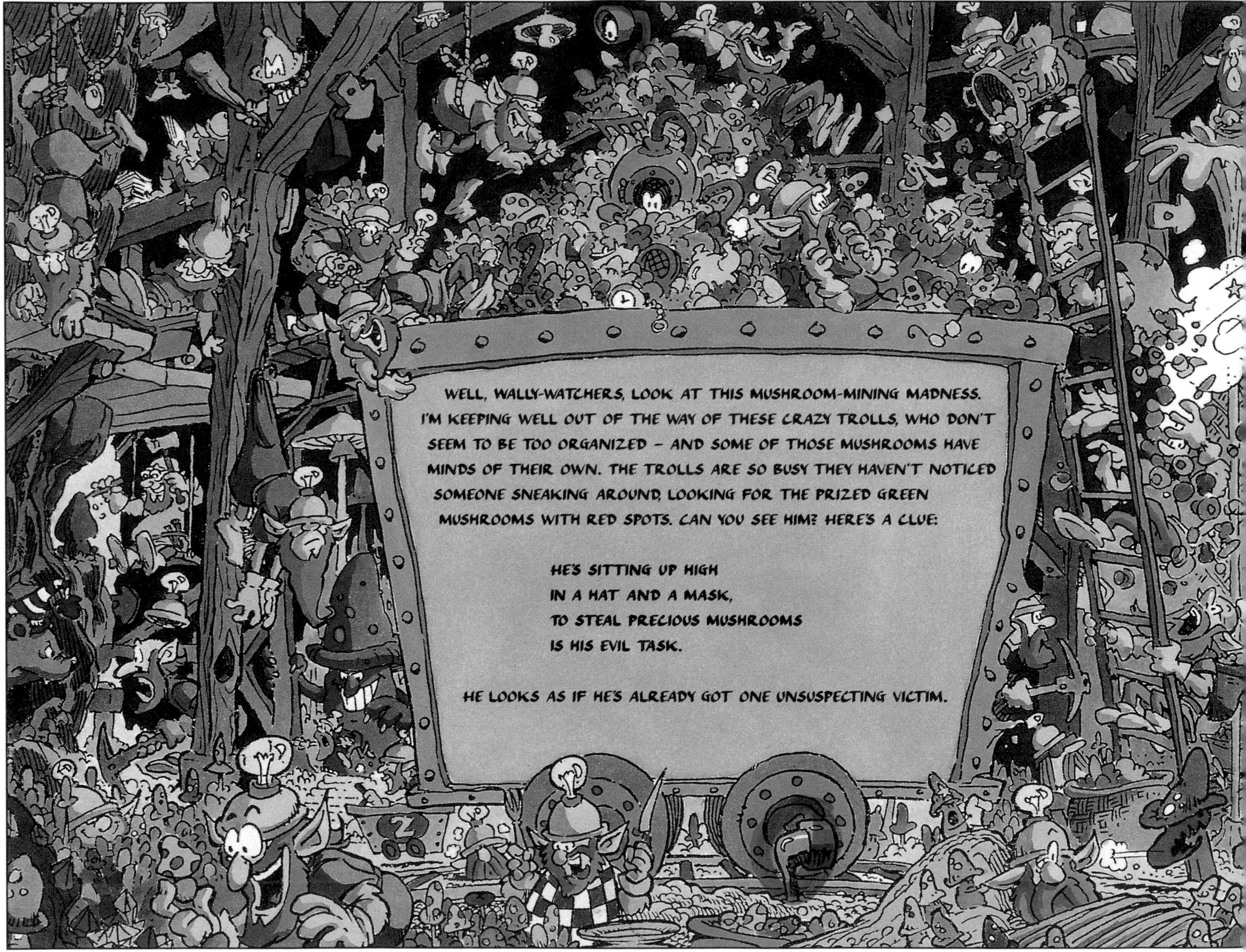

WELL, WALLY-WATCHERS, LOOK AT THIS MUSHROOM-MINING MADNESS.
I'M KEEPING WELL OUT OF THE WAY OF THESE CRAZY TROLLS, WHO DON'T
SEEM TO BE TOO ORGANIZED – AND SOME OF THOSE MUSHROOMS HAVE
MINDS OF THEIR OWN. THE TROLLS ARE SO BUSY THEY HAVEN'T NOTICED
SOMEONE SNEAKING AROUND, LOOKING FOR THE PRIZED GREEN
MUSHROOMS WITH RED SPOTS. CAN YOU SEE HIM? HERE'S A CLUE:

HE'S SITTING UP HIGH
IN A HAT AND A MASK,
TO STEAL PRECIOUS MUSHROOMS
IS HIS EVIL TASK.

HE LOOKS AS IF HE'S ALREADY GOT ONE UNSUSPECTING VICTIM.

MUSHROOM-MINING TROLLS

CAN YOU FIND A VICIOUS RED MUSHROOM, A RED AND ORANGE STRIPED MUSHROOM AND 9 RARE GREEN MUSHROOMS WITH RED SPOTS LIKE THE ONE BELOW?

WHEN YOU'VE FOUND ALL THESE TRY SAYING THIS TONGUE-TWISTER REALLY FAST WHILE WORKING OUT THE QUICKEST ROUTE TO THE MUSHROOM IN THE MIDDLE OF THE MAZE.

MRS MISSION MASHING MUSHROOMS

DID YOU KNOW?

Mushrooms are a fungus, made up mostly of water.

There are more than 70 species of poisonous mushrooms – some of them are deadly!

The largest recorded tree fungus has a circumference of 409 cm.

THINGS TO DO

Here are 4 pieces of picture. 2 belong to this page and 2 come from somewhere else in the book. Can you find exactly where they come from?

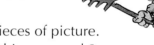

A   B

C   D

How would you know you had a toadstool in your dustbin?

There wouldn't be mushroom inside.

SNAKE PIT

- [ ] A snake in a bow tie
- [ ] A green scarf
- [ ] A snakey hat
- [ ] 15 blue Hunter hats
- [ ] A snake with white spots
- [ ] A blue scarf
- [ ] A winking snake
- [ ] A snake seeing stars
- [ ] A little blue snake
- [ ] 3 shields

CAVE RAVE

- [ ] A square wheel
- [ ] 2 washing lines
- [ ] Rock drawings
- [ ] A hungry baby mammoth
- [ ] A fish skeleton
- [ ] A rose
- [ ] A bird's nest
- [ ] A walking stick
- [ ] A money bag
- [ ] A worm

DINOSAUR GAMES

- [ ] 3 scrolls
- [ ] 4 bobble hats
- [ ] A blue beetle
- [ ] Wally's walking stick
- [ ] 2 pairs of glasses
- [ ] A yellow tree lizard
- [ ] A coconut tree
- [ ] Dinosaur twins
- [ ] A duckling
- [ ] A watch

FILM SET

- [ ] Tarzan
- [x] The Tin Man
- [ ] Laurel & Hardy
- [ ] A flying saucer
- [x] 2 Draculas
- [ ] The Invisible Man
- [ ] Robin Hood
- [ ] Charlie Chaplin
- [ ] A red spaceman
- [ ] A smiling face badge

DRAGON RIDE

- [x] A magnifying glass
- [x] A watch
- [x] 3 mice
- [x] A periscope
- [x] Envelopes
- [x] 3 clocks
- [x] 2 fireman's hosepipes
- [x] 2 playing cards
- [x] Traffic lights
- [x] 6 arrows

MEDIEVAL MAYHEM

- [ ] 2 firemen
- [ ] A jester
- [ ] A tin can
- [ ] A feather
- [ ] A parachutist
- [ ] A dustbin
- [ ] A chef
- [ ] 2 tennis balls
- [ ] An alarm clock
- [ ] A cake

ICE-CREAM PARTY

- [ ] 6 ice-cream cornets
- [ ] A sleeping pig
- [ ] A spanner
- [ ] A screwdriver
- [ ] A boot
- [ ] A long fork
- [ ] A checked hanky
- [ ] A furry spaceman
- [ ] An empty bottle
- [ ] A glass of chocolate milk

A FEAST OF PIES

- [ ] A chipped plate
- [ ] A green bowl
- [ ] 6 red neck-scarves
- [ ] A flying flan tin
- [ ] A yellow neck-scarf
- [ ] 22 cherries
- [ ] A green neck-scarf
- [ ] A cake slice
- [ ] A blue saucer
- [ ] 3 striped tablecloths

BALLOON RACE

- [ ] 3 star-studded balloons
- [x] 2 elephants
- [x] 2 walking sticks
- [x] 4 wasps
- [ ] A policeman
- [ ] An ostrich
- [ ] A pirate
- [ ] 2 teacups and saucers
- [ ] A bird's nest
- [ ] A clown

SNOWSTORM

- [ ] A broomstick
- [ ] 15 scarves
- [ ] A toboggan
- [ ] A bow tie
- [ ] 2 saucepans
- [ ] 2 twiggy heads
- [ ] A red jacket
- [ ] 2 top hats
- [ ] A pear
- [ ] A pipe

WILD WEST HEROES

- [ ] A spider's web
- [ ] A snake
- [ ] A bath brush
- [ ] 6 green statues
- [ ] A gold pot
- [ ] An alarm clock
- [ ] 3 arrows
- [ ] A cat
- [ ] A mouse
- [ ] 8 sheriff badges

PIRATES AHOY

- [ ] 3 pearl necklaces
- [ ] 10 daggers and cutlasses
- [ ] 4 pink diamonds
- [ ] A teddy
- [ ] A skeleton
- [ ] 2 spotted handkerchiefs
- [ ] 3 striped hats
- [ ] A cannonball
- [ ] An anchor
- [ ] A seagull

STAR GAZING

- [ ] 19 yellow stars
- [ ] A cup and saucer
- [ ] 2 buckets
- [ ] A 4-eyed creature
- [ ] An astronaut sitting on a sign
- [ ] A crash-landing
- [ ] An octopus
- [ ] A family of yellow bugs
- [ ] A space garage
- [ ] A spoon

MUSHROOM-MINING TROLLS

- [ ] A walking stick
- [ ] 2 red bottles
- [ ] 2 pairs of glasses
- [ ] A rake
- [x] 2 periscopes
- [ ] A bossy green mushroom
- [ ] 3 blue forks
- [ ] A reading troll
- [ ] A tin can
- [x] A pair of binoculars

CUPID CHAOS

- [ ] 2 ladybirds
- [ ] A snail
- [ ] 12 red hearts
- [ ] A unicorn
- [ ] A yellow and blue butterfly
- [ ] A mouse
- [ ] A pink rabbit
- [ ] A fox
- [ ] 10 Cupids
- [ ] A yellow duck

DEEP SEA DIVING

- [ ] A periscope
- [ ] A wristwatch
- [ ] A sausage
- [ ] 5 rings
- [ ] A broken watch
- [ ] 4 bobble hats
- [ ] A pipe
- [ ] A scroll
- [ ] A walking stick
- [ ] 4 fish hooks

ANSWERS

DINOSAUR GAMES

Riddle: There is a tennis ball in the nest by the purple, sleeping dinosaur.

The daft dino is made up like this:
  beak and crest – Pteranodon
  head – Triceratops
  neck – Apatosaurus
  legs and body – Tyrannosaurus
  sail – Dimetrodon
  tail – Stegosaurus.

Misfit: A bird from Cupid Chaos

MEDIEVAL MAYHEM

Riddle: The rolling pin is falling from the battlements on the far left of the picture.

D is the odd picture out.

Misfit: A tiger from Cave Rave

SNAKE PIT

Riddle: The yellow snake is on the floor in the middle of the picture.

Snake A is the longest.

There are 9 different snakes – adder, boa constrictor, cobra, grass snake, anaconda, rattlesnake, viper, asp, python.

Misfit: Mushroom from Mining Trolls

FILM SET

Riddle: The prop is a white piano underneath the text.

The names are: Sinbad, Aladdin, Mowgli, Tarzan, Dracula and the piece of equipment is a clapperboard.

Misfit: Space baby from Star Gazing

ICE-CREAM PARTY

Riddle: The most popular flavour is banana and marmalade.

The ice-cream flavours are: parsnip, broccoli, tomato, cabbage and carrot.

The pudding pairs are:
  strawberries and cream,
  pancakes and syrup,
  jelly and ice-cream,
  bananas and custard.

Misfit: A fish from Deep Sea Diving

CAVE RAVE

Riddle: The mammoth is about to tread on a drawing pin.

The letters left over spell Mad Rock Street.

Misfit: A cake from A Feast of Pies

DRAGON RIDE

Riddle: There is a yellow key just above the dragon's head.

Hunter B has a different moustache and Hunter C has a different hat.

	M	E	D	U	S	A	
	M	E	R	M	A	I	D
		S	A	T	Y	R	
		P	E	G	A	S	U	S
U	N	I	C	O	R	N	
	M	I	N	O	T	A	U	R

Misfit: Dinosaur from Dinosaur Games

A FEAST OF PIES

Riddle: He's an icing-sugar man, sitting between two sets of steps.

Grains: barley, oats, wheat, millet, rye.

Misfit: Bowl from Ice-Cream Party

BALLOON RACE

Riddle: He's a frog and the number on his balloon is 28.

The highest number is 747.

Picture C is the odd one out and can be found on the Film Set.

Misfit: A mouse from Dragon Ride

PIRATES AHOY

Riddle: The pirate's name is Flora and she's swinging from the rigging.

As for the treasure: "It's in the crow's nest"

Misfit: Birds from Film Set

CUPID CHAOS

Riddle: The tortoise and the hare are in the bottom left-hand corner.

This square is exactly the same as the original:

The saying in code is: Elephants never forget.

Misfit: A snake from Snake Pit

SNOWSTORM

Riddle: There is a snowman with his head on upside down, just under the text.

A, B & E complete the snowhead.

Misfit: A boot from Wild West Heroes

STAR GAZING

Riddle: The little Martians are in a yellow space-craft just above the big green planet.

The signpost says: Welcome to outer space.

Misfit: A balloon from Balloon Race

DEEP SEA DIVING

Riddle: There is a submarine in the bottom left-hand corner, just above the treasure chest.

The seahorse differences are: nose, horn on the head, tongue, back fin, bottom fin, tail.

	S	T	A	R	F	I	S	H
	N	E	T					
	S	C	R	O	L	L		
	S	H	E	L	L			
H	O	O	K					
	T	R	E	A	S	U	R	E

Misfit: A diver from Medieval Mayhem

WILD WEST HEROES

Riddle: There is a vase just about to drop from the saloon.

Rope D will unravel the villain.

The pickaxe is the odd silhouette. It can be found on Mushroom-Mining Trolls.

Misfit: A top hat from Snowstorm

MUSHROOM-MINING TROLLS

Riddle: The masked marauder is up on a beam in the top left-hand corner.

A & D are on this page, B comes from Wild West Heroes and C from Pirates Ahoy.

Misfit: Choking man from Pirates Ahoy

AND FINALLY

Woof and Wizard Whitebeard appear in Film Set. The striped sock is in Cave Rave and the striped tie in Dragon Ride. There are 4 bananas in Film Set, 3 in Cave Rave, 1 in Dragon Ride, 1 in Snowstorm and 2 in Mushroom-Mining Trolls.

With special thanks to Stephen Martiniere and Greg Dubuque
First published 1994 by Walker Books Ltd
87 Vauxhall Walk, London SE11 5HJ

2 3 4 5 6 7 8 9 10

Text © 1994 Martin Handford

The right of Martin Handford to be identified as author of this work has been asserted by him in accordance with the Copyright, Designs and Patents Act 1988.

King Kong © 1933 RKO Pictures, Inc. All Rights Reserved. Courtesy of Turner Entertainment Co.

This book has been typeset in Optima.

Printed in England

British Library Cataloguing in Publication Data
A catalogue record for this book is available from the British Library.

ISBN 0-7445-3676-6